Christ's Own Forever

Episcopal Baptism of Infants and Young Children

Parent/Godparent Journal

by Mary Lee Wile

Morehouse Education Resources
A division of Church Publishing Incorporated

600 Grant Street, Suite 630
Denver, CO 80203

Morehouse Education Resources
a division of Church Publishing Incorporated
Editorial Offices
600 Grant Street, Suite 630
Denver, CO 80203

James R. Creasey, Publisher

Liz Riggleman, Editor

Regan MacStravic, Photography

Sue MacStravic, Cover Design

Printed in the United States of America.

ISBN 978-1-9319-6003-8

Dear Parent or Godparent,

May God's gracious love for you and for the child you bring to baptism guide, sustain, and bless you.

You are embarking on a journey of faith, responsible not only for your own spiritual wellbeing, but for your child's or godchild's spiritual nurture now as well. This journal is designed to help you prepare for the baptism—and beyond. Part of the preparation is self-examination, a chance to think about your own religious background, your spiritual journey, your current beliefs, dreams, hopes and fears. Another part of the preparation focuses specifically on the child.

The final part of the journal looks beyond baptism, asking you to consider ways of helping your child or godchild live into the baptismal vows you will make on his or her behalf.

You may be asked to look at certain parts of the journal before meeting with the clergy or layperson who will oversee the final preparation and/or follow-up for the sacrament of Holy Baptism. Read through the passages and questions, even if you don't have time to answer them all. It may be that you will feel called to respond in depth—or it may be that you will come back and answer some questions six months or even a year later.

If this is the second or more time you have brought a child to be baptized, you may find that you are called to different questions, and that your answers change as the family grows or the number of godchildren increases. Trust the Holy Spirit to guide you in your interaction with this journal.

Take seriously the vows you will make, and be intentional in honoring them through involving your child or godchild in a life of prayer and communal worship. One of the gifts of baptism is that it brings the child into the wider church family. Never feel that you are in the business of parenting or godparenting alone.

Use this journal as a way of acknowledging and deepening your own spirituality, and as a resource for helping your child or god-child develop a deeply grounded spiritual life as a beloved child of God.

O God, you have taught us through your blessed Son that whoever receives a little child in the name of Christ receives Christ himself: We give you thanks for the blessing you have bestowed upon this family in giving them a child. Confirm their joy by a lively sense of your presence with them, and give them calm strength and patient wisdom as they seek to bring this child to love all that is true and noble, just and pure, lovable and gracious, excellent and admirable, following the example of our Lord and Savior, Jesus Christ. Amen. (The Book of Common Prayer, *p. 443*)

Mary Lee Wile
August 15, 2002

Pastoral Introduction to Baptism from Common Worship: Services and Prayers for the Church of England

Baptism marks the beginning of a journey with God which continues for the rest of our lives, the first step in response to God's love. For all involved, particularly the candidates but also parents, godparents and sponsors, it is a joyful moment when we rejoice in what God has done for us in Christ, making serious promises and declaring the faith. The wider community of the local church and friends welcome the new Christian, promising support and prayer for the future. Hearing and doing these things provides an opportunity to remember our own baptism and reflect on the progress made on that journey, which is now to be shared with this new member of the Church.

The service paints many vivid pictures of what happens on the Christian way. There is the sign of the cross, the badge of faith in the Christian journey, which reminds us of Christ's death for us. Our 'drowning' in the water of baptism, where we believe we die to sin and are raised to new life, unites us to Christ's dying and rising, a picture that can be brought home vividly by the way the baptism is administered. Water is also a sign of new life, as we are born again by water and the Spirit, as Jesus was at his baptism. And as a sign of that new life, there may be a lighted candle, a picture of the light of Christ conquering the darkness of evil. Everyone who is baptized walks in that light for the rest of their lives.

As you pray for the candidates, picture them with yourself and the whole Church throughout the ages, journeying into the fullness of God's love.

Jesus said, 'I came that they may have life, and have it abundantly.'

John 10:10

Prologue A:
Choosing Godparents

As a parent, you have the awesome responsibility of selecting those who will be an integral part of your child's spiritual growth. In years past, godparents were also expected to become the primary care-takers of a godchild whose parents died or became incapacitated; although this custodial aspect is no longer an assumed part of godparenting, the tradition serves to indicate the importance of choosing people you can trust with your child's immortal soul.

Choose prayerfully.

The Rev. Paige Blair, rector of St. George's in York Harbor, Maine offers the following guidelines: choose persons of integrity who experience God within a Christian community and who ask the questions, "Who is God, who is Christ in my life?" In other words, choose people who are committed, thoughtful Christians, people who are not afraid to ask questions, whose faith is living and active.

Blair says that over the past 10 years, parents have asked if Jewish or Muslim friends could serve as godparents, and she has gently pointed out that asking them to commit to the Baptismal Covenant on behalf of the child would be asking them to dishonor their own faith commitments. We need to respect our friends' religious integrity. Ask them, Blair says, to be spiritual mentors and friends, but not godparents.

That doesn't, however, mean that all godparents need to be alike. Just as families come in diverse configurations, so do godparents.

Brother Eldridge Pendleton of the Society of St. John the Evangelist is a godparent six times over. As a celibate monk, being a godfather is immensely gratifying: "it gives the childless children. It's really important for those who, for whatever reason, don't have children." In other words, you needn't choose people who are "parents" to be your child's godparents. It's far more important to choose someone with whom your child will feel safe and comfortable sharing faith issues and struggles as the years go by.

Choose people you respect, people you want in relationship with your child. What you ask of godparents is both an honor and a responsibility. Baptism is a social occasion, yes, a public welcoming of people into the family of the Church, but it is far more: it is a deeply holy time during which you and the godparents will make solemn vows on behalf of your child.

Once you have carefully, prayerfully chosen godparents for your child, and they have said yes, thank them.

And over the months and years ahead, keep them involved in your child's life. They are intimately and forever a part of your extended family.

Prologue B:
Being a Godparent

Before standing up there in front of God and every-
body and taking solemn baptismal vows on behalf of
this child, ask yourself: "Am I sure I want to do this?"

You have been deeply honored by being asked to enter
into this relationship; you will be entrusted with the
care and nurture of a human soul; you will promise to
be responsible for seeing that the child "is brought up
in the Christian faith and life."

Being a godparent is a lifelong commitment; it doesn't end with
confirmation. You can't "divorce" your godchild. When my own
godmother died several years ago, she even bequeathed me some of
her books. Our relationship transcended death.

Br. Eldridge Pendleton delights in the role. "It's such a privilege,"
he says. "As a godparent, I just feel so connected to those people."

The Rev. Daniel Warren, rector of St. Paul's in Brunswick, Maine
talks of the special nature of the relationship between godparent
and godchild because godparents "don't keep score or grade their
godchildren;" there can be an ease between them that is rare in our
competitive culture. Besides being a responsibility, godparenting
can also be a joy.

If you can, after prayerful consideration, say yes to being a godparent, honor your commitment by going thoughtfully through this
journal and by attending the preparatory sessions along with the

parent(s) and child. Spend time familiarizing yourself with the baptismal service itself. Hold the child and talk or read aloud; let the child hear your voice.

Once the service is over, your new life as godparent really begins. Stay in close touch with the child's family. If you live at a distance, send e-mail or letters. On the anniversary of the baptism, send a card to the child. If you live close enough, help plan a celebration for the anniversary—year by year by year. As years pass, direct those e-mails and letters to the child rather than the parent(s). Let your godchild know you: invite the child into your spiritual life; share your ideas; converse about God. If you can afford to do so, send a gift on each anniversary of baptism. Br. Eldridge says, "It's so much fun picking out books each year" for his diverse godchildren, and I will suggest later in the journal that books with stories from Scripture make particularly appropriate presents from godparents. Elaine Ramshaw's *The Godparent Book* offers a wide selection of activities and ideas for living into your new role.

The best gift you can give your godchild, however, is the gift of your own life experiences as a struggling Christian. Be available as your godchild grows; remain part of the extended family that surrounds the child.

And know that you, too, remain forever a beloved child of God.

Part I:
Preparation

The "Why" of Baptism

Every morning when I come downstairs,
my first stop is at the icon of our Lord that
hangs next to a photograph of my children
when they were little. Every morning I ask a
blessing, and then I close my prayers by making the sign of the cross
on my children's foreheads, repeating words from the baptismal
service: "you are sealed by the Holy Spirit in baptism and marked
as Christ's own forever." Although my children are grown and gone
now into the fullness of their own lives, they remain not only my
children, but God's. In this troubling and uncertain world, their
eternal adoption into God's family through the waters of baptism
matters deeply. As the apostle Paul reminded the Romans, "nothing
can separate us from the love of God in Christ Jesus our Lord." My
morning ritual reminds me that my children are held in the heart of
God, incorporated into the Body of Christ, and that nothing—not
even death—can separate them from the love of God.

You hold this journal in your hands because you have begun the
process of preparing for your child's or godchild's baptism. You
have said "yes" to the promptings of your own heart and perhaps
to the encouragement of friends or relatives. Baptism used to be a
societal norm, something that was automatically "done" to a child.
In the early years of this new millennium, however, saying yes to
baptism is a different, deeper choice.

Spend some time pondering what led you to seek Holy Baptism for your child, or, if you are to be a godparent, what led you to accept that role:

....

....

....

....

....

Priest and professor John Westerhoff writes that, "It is God who is the prior actor in baptism, an action to which we can only respond." In other words, according to Westerhoff, no matter what other reasons you might name, one reason that you have engaged in this preparatory process is that God invited you and, on behalf of the child, you said yes. With that thought in mind, what stand out as specific moments or significant events in which you sensed God's presence or God's action in your life, moving you toward this place in your journey, this choice for your child or godchild?

....

....

....

....

....

....

In saying yes to baptism, just what is it that you have undertaken on behalf of your child? What is Holy Baptism? If you look at page 298 in *The Book of Common Prayer*, the official rubrics tell us that "Holy Baptism is full initiation by water and the Holy Spirit into Christ's Body the Church. The bond which God establishes in baptism is indissoluble." What that means is that through baptism, your child becomes part of an extended family of fellow-Christians; your child enters a covenanted relationship with God.

People used to fear that the unbaptized remained exiled from God and could never attain salvation; more recent readings of Scripture recognize that God's love extends to all people. Baptism doesn't make God love you or your child more; what it does is to name and sanctify the relationship between God and the one being baptized. "What God does in Holy Baptism is nothing less than to adopt a human being to be forever His own child," asserts The Rev. Dr. Carroll Simcox, past rector of St. Thomas in New York City.

I remember a friend asking me, when our firstborn children were about six months old, "Do you think we'll spend as much time with the second ones, just watching them sleep?" (Yes, we did...) Spend some time just holding and looking at your child, thinking and perhaps even saying aloud, "You are a beloved child of God." (If you are to be the child's godparent, this is equally important—as a practical matter of having the child become accustomed to your voice and your presence before the actual service, and as a spiritual matter of acknowledging your prayerful connection to the child.) Then spend some time thinking and writing about the hopes and dreams you have for this child, and how you see baptism being part of those dreams.

. . . .

. . . .

. . . .

. . . .

. . . .

One of my seminary professors used to say, "God is as real as gravity."
Robert Sherman spoke of baptism as an absolute, grounded reality in
which a person is marked and sealed as God's own. The English mystic
Julian of Norwich wrote that "God stands nearer to us than our own
soul, for he is the ground on which we stand." Spend some time pondering those things which ground *you*, which keep you focused and
centered. For some it may be family or friends, for others the work
you do each day, for some it may be athletic or artistic endeavors.
Some of you may look at this child and feel grounded in a new way.
Make a list, and then consider how these are gifts God offers to and
through you.

. . . .

. . . .

. . . .

. . . .

. . . .

. . . .

. . . .

. . . .

Remember that it is through you that your child or godchild will find
solid ground, and by answering God's invitation to baptize this child,
you offer deep, abiding grounding.

By Water and the Holy Spirit: The "What" of Baptism

Just prior to the actual baptism (on pages 306-307 in *The Book of Common Prayer*) the priest will offer thanksgiving over the water:

> *We thank you, Almighty God, for the gift of water. Over it the Holy Spirit moved in the beginning of creation. Through it you led the children of Israel out of their bondage in Egypt into the land of promise. In it your Son Jesus received the baptism of John and was anointed by the Holy Spirit as the Messiah, the Christ, to lead us, through his death and resurrection, from the bondage of sin into everlasting life.*

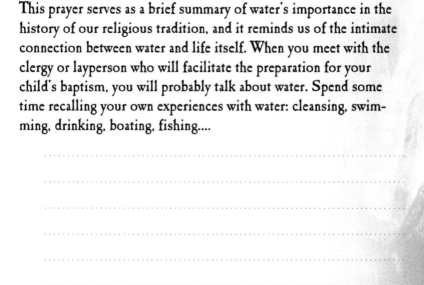

This prayer serves as a brief summary of water's importance in the history of our religious tradition, and it reminds us of the intimate connection between water and life itself. When you meet with the clergy or layperson who will facilitate the preparation for your child's baptism, you will probably talk about water. Spend some time recalling your own experiences with water: cleansing, swimming, drinking, boating, fishing....

The Rev. Daniel Warren, rector of St. Paul's in Brunswick, Maine speaks of the "aha!" we feel when we come to a body of water; paleontologist Jane Goodall once said that even chimpanzees dance with awe at the sight of a waterfall. I remember having lived away from the ocean for 12 years and then arriving at water's edge: I kicked off my shoes and walked into the surf fully clothed, my children following.

Can you recall "aha!" moments connected with water?

. . . .

. . . .

. . . .

. . . .

. . . .

. . . .

Some denominations still practice full immersion baptism; even within the Episcopal Church there are times and places where older candidates are taken to rivers or lakes or ocean for baptism. Most of the time, however, what happens is that the blessed water is poured or sprinkled three times over the person being baptized (replicating the "pouring out" of the Spirit). The priest (or other person performing the actual baptism) will call your child by name, and then say, "I baptize you in the Name of the Father, and of the Son, and of the Holy Spirit. Amen."

Besides being the source of life and providing restoration and renewal for the human spirit, water can also serve as a boundary. The Piscataqua River, for example, separates Maine from New Hampshire at its southern border. The Rio Grande divides countries. And in our own salvation history, crossing the Jordan into the promised land holds powerful associations of achieving freedom and peace. Just so is baptism a crossing over into the promises of Christ, into the household of God.

What are times in your life when you can recognize having made a transition, crossed over a boundary, gained new freedom (and with it, perhaps, new responsibilities)?

....

....

....

....

....

....

....

You are to be commended for trusting your child to this journey through the waters of baptism. The language of what happens can be frightening: you send your child through death into resurrection and rebirth. The Rev. John Westerhoff notes that in some traditions the child is literally carried into the church in a small coffin, acknowledging that the child will die with Christ before being reborn. The Thanksgiving over Water continues:

> *We thank you, Father, for the water of Baptism. In it we are buried with Christ in his death. By it we share in his resurrection. Through it we are reborn by the Holy Spirit. Therefore in joyful obedience to your Son, we bring into his fellowship those who come to him in faith, baptizing them in the Name of the Father, and of the Son, and of the Holy Spirit.*

When the one baptizing plunges his or her hand into the font, breaking the water, this is the necessary preliminary action for the rebirth of baptism.

Take some time to recall your child's actual moment of birth, or for adoptive parents or for godparents, the first moment you held the child in your arms.

....

....

....

....

....

....

....

Besides water baptism, your child will also experience consignation: the priest will make the sign of the cross on your child's forehead (often using holy oil), again calling the child by name and saying, "you are sealed by the Holy Spirit in baptism and marked as Christ's own forever."

As theology professor Ellen Charry explains, what happens is that "They are grafted into the divine life, sanctified by being chrismated—signed with oil—by the Holy Spirit and marked as Christ's own forever." This action provides your child a new identity, as with the wax of a signet ring or even the branding of cattle, a permanent mark of ownership: your child will enter forever the extended Christian family. Your child will belong to Christ.

This doesn't mean, however, that the beloved individuality of the child is subsumed; it is enhanced by being part of this lively, loving, diverse, and contentious family: "It is important to say that the human spirit is awakened by the coming of the Holy Spirit, but never overwhelmed or extinguished," writes Marianne Micks in *Deep Waters*.

What individual and unique traits do you already see emerging in this child?

....

....

....

....

....

....

....

....

In John's gospel, the evangelist uses the word "paraclete" for the Holy Spirit, which Micks translates as "one called alongside," the one who will be with this child always as a companion, an "intercessor, support, or counselor." Think of the comfort in that reality: sealing with the Holy Spirit is an overt promise that this child will never be alone, but will forever be companioned by God's Holy Spirit.

Name some times in your own life when you have felt isolated and alone, and then note what happened to get you through those times. In retrospect, can you recognize God's companionship in any of your examples?

....
....
....
....
....
....

Families offer some of our deepest companionship experiences.
Think about the immediate family in which this child will grow up.
Describe your own concept of what it means to be part of a family
(remembering how the late 20th Century has expanded our understanding and definition of "family):

....
....
....
....
....
....

Now think about your experiences with the Church, the Body of
Christ, the *extended family* into which you are bringing your child
through baptism.

....
....
....
....

Some of your memories may be comforting, joyful ones; others may be less so. Just as our own families can be full of both love and tension, so can the Christian family; Paul's letters let us listen in on disagreements going on nearly 2000 years ago. And yet, all these centuries later, this extended Christian family still embraces us. "Christianity," writes William Willimon in *What's Right with the Church?*, "is not a home correspondence course in salvation. This religion is anything but a private affair." Community is the heart of it. Look again at the Baptismal Service. On page 303 the presider will ask the people in the congregation if they will promise to support your child in his or her faith journey, and they will vow to be a part of the child's growth and nurture in the Church.

Patricia Bamforth, active laywoman and grandmother, speaks of "incredible relief" when her first child was baptized: "I wasn't in it alone any more." Her fears and concerns and joys and questions as a new parent were shared with the whole parish—and with God. "Being with a supportive community is *so* important," she says.

What are your own fears and concerns and joys and questions—and how do you hope the Church can share them, maybe even help answer some of them?

By water and the Holy Spirit, your child or godchild will become a baptized Christian. From the language of the service, it's clear that baptism isn't an end in itself. It is permanent and indissoluble—baptism is forever—but it is also only the beginning: "Baptism is more than a momentary act; it is the beginning of a lifelong pilgrimage," Westerhoff reminds us. "My *vocation*," says Episcopal priest, professor, and writer Barbara Brown Taylor, "is to be God's person in the world.... The instant we rise dripping from the waters of baptism and the sign of the cross is made upon our foreheads, we are marked as Christ's own forever." Note some ways in which you have been "God's person in the world," ways in which you have lived out your own covenant with God, times when you felt most fully yourself, living out and into your God-given potential.

....

....

....

....

....

....

What are some specific ways in which you, as parent or godparent, might foster your child's or godchild's full potential as an individual, and as a Christian?

....

....

....

....

....

....

"To be called of God takes time, and to answer takes even more time," writes Sam Portaro in *Crossing the Jordan*. You don't have to do this all at once, just day by day by day.

I once heard of a monk who looked himself in the mirror every morning and said, "I will begin again today to be a Christian." Each day is a good day to begin.

Promises: Promises We Make to Our Children

"The child in baptism begins his Christian life as one who must live by the faith and love of others," says Carroll Simcox. You, as parent or godparent, are among the most significant "others" in this child's life in faith. What you do, or don't do, matters. Are there specific (either overt or implicit) promises that you have already made to this child, yourself, your spouse, your partner, a friend, or God that are connected with the child's *physical* wellbeing?

....
....
....
....
....
....
....
....

Have you already also made promises that concern your child's or god-child's *spiritual* wellbeing? (You will do so at baptism, remember.)

....

....

....

....

....

....

In our secular culture, a question that you are likely to encounter from friends or family not connected with the Church is why you are offering your child for adoption by God into the Christian family. Why does it matter that you raise this child to know and love God? Ellen Charry answers by saying that "knowing and loving God is the mechanism of choice for forming excellence of character and promoting genuine happiness." In other words, knowing and loving God is good for us; it makes us better, stronger people—and it makes people genuinely happy. Prayers from the Baptismal Service acknowledge this: "Give [this child] an inquiring and discerning heart, a spirit to know and to love you, and the gift of joy and wonder in all your works."

By saying yes to baptism for your child or godchild, you offer life and hope and courage and joy. And you promise to help along the way.

Read the actual promises you will make at baptism on your child's behalf (see pages 301-303 in *The Book of Common Prayer*). You will begin by agreeing, with God's help, to bring up the child "in the Christian faith and life...by your prayers and witness [to] help this child grow into the full stature of Christ." And in order to do so, you then will make a series of promises.

Spend some time pondering these promises. Consider what it means, for example, to "renounce Satan and all the spiritual forces of wickedness...the evil powers of this world...all sinful desires..." When you think of wickedness and sin and evil, what memories or images come to mind? And what does it feel like to imagine renouncing them on behalf of this child?

After the renunciations, you will then respond "I do" when asked if you will promise to "turn to Jesus Christ...put your whole trust in his grace and love... follow and obey him as your Lord." How do those promises resonate with you? What does it mean to you to turn to Christ, to trust and follow him? Is turning to Christ, trusting and following him, already a familiar response for you, or will learning to do so feel new?

Some of these promises and vows may feel harder than others. To whom will you turn for help in keeping them? (It's good to have ideas ahead of time; hard times or confusing times or dark times always come, times when we need help.) (Yes, God will be there, too, but remember that God often works through the hands and hearts of others.)

....

....

....

....

....

....

By opening your family or your heart to this child, you implicitly promise love. By bringing this child to baptism, you promise a life of faith. Salvadoran Archbishop Oscar Romero said that "Faith is what a child has when its father puts out his hands and says, 'Jump!' and the child leaps into space with the assurance that its father's hands won't let it fall..." Romero offers hope to those who "even in the darkest time" keep their faith and find assurance in Christ's loving embrace. On the other hand, "those who won't leap into Christ's arms because they are more anchored to their earthly things, those who don't trust in God, those who don't believe that God goes with our history and is going to save us" are at the mercy of contemporary culture and its violence, greed, and underlying despair.

Popular culture, Charry says, "plays on cynicism, despair, and distrust." Taylor warns that slick advertisements "appeal to the same part of us, the hunger to be safe, to be happy, to be loved, that holy images do, and in many ways the ongoing struggle of faith is the struggle to choose between those that have the power to save us and those that do not." As parent or godparent, your implied promise is to help this child locate love and security and happiness in the intimacy of family and in the wider embrace of the Church. The glittering material world sings its siren songs even to the very young. Sing lullabies, say daily prayers, read good books aloud, take the child to church and out into the world of nature. Lay down patterns of words and sounds and ideas that will provide safe harbor for the child during times of trial and temptation.

What are some of your own early memories of prayers or songs or books or nature?

....

....

....

....

....

....

What are some of your early memories of advertisements and other What are some of your early memories of advertisements and other secular messages?

....

....

....

....

....

....

The Rev. Vicki Sirota, who serves Holy Nativity Church in inner city Baltimore, talks earnestly about the importance of having children memorize passages of Scripture, prayers, and hymns as antidotes to the dangerous, violent culture that surrounds them.

What do you want to be sure your child or godchild hears and knows? From what would you like to protect this child?

....

....

....

....

....

....

....

The daughter of a dear friend grew up listening to her mother's daily recitation of Evening Prayer, and one evening as she looked out the window at a golden Colorado sunset, she exclaimed. "O gracious light!" For two-year old Rachel, what she saw was more than just a pretty sky; her sensibilities had been informed by her mother's daily reading of the Evening Prayer service from *The Book of Common Prayer*, and what Rachel saw was God's gracious hand at work.

The Rev. Paige Blair insists, "There is no such thing as an atheist. You will have a god. It's how human beings are made. It may be God Almighty, or it may be a god of your own choosing and making, but it will exercise the same control." One of Bob Dylan's songs reminds us of the same thing: "It may be the devil or it may be the Lord, but you're gonna have to serve somebody."

What have been the "gods" you've served over the years? Where has God fit in?

_____

_____

_____

_____

_____

_____

_____

Always keep in mind that what you are doing by arranging your child's baptism is offering this child the best life you can. Through your promise to "be responsible for seeing that the child you present is brought up in the Christian faith and life," you place your child in the loving service of Christ.

The "Collect for Peace" from Morning Prayer which I recite on my way to school each day says "to know you is eternal life and to serve you is perfect freedom." Americans are taught to be autonomous, independent, and self-serving, and yet the counter-cultural Christian message is that life and joy and even freedom lie instead in the life of faithful service to God.

When you think of the word "freedom," what comes to mind?

_____

_____

_____

_____

_____

_____

When you pair the word "freedom" with your child or godchild, what ideas or dreams or fears come to mind?

....

....

....

....

....

....

Are there other promises, spiritual or physical or emotional, that you have made or intend to make to your child or godchild?

....

....

....

....

....

Promises: God's Promises to Us and to Our Children

"What is the most important spiritual gift that we can pass on to our children?" ask Ellen and Dana Charry. "They need the power of God, the armor of Christ, and the knowledge that their bodies are tem- ples of the Holy Spirit." They need to know that they are firmly and forever marked and sealed as Christ's own. They need to know that God's promise holds.

Presiding Bishop Frank Griswold writes that growing into baptism "shows forth God's yearning for our good and our flourishing, which lies at the heart of what we call God's will." Charry echoes this by insisting that "God is committed to human flourishing." Both emphasize that baptism includes not only our promises to God, but God's promises to us, God's desire that we flourish.

Perhaps the most beloved verse in the New Testament is John 3:16, which begins, "God so loved the world..." God's promise is to love us.

"To believe in Jesus is to believe that Jesus is the Son of God and that God loved the world so much that God gave the Son as a gift. The God revealed in Jesus is a God whose love knows no bounds and who asks only that one receive the gift," writes Professor Gail O'Day in the *New Interpreter's Bible*.

What are times throughout your life when you have felt most deeply loved? What were the specific circumstances that allowed you to receive that love?

....

....

....

....

....

....

....

In any of those instances, were you aware of love bigger than the moment, of something you might call the love of God?

....

....

....

....

....

....

....

Saying that baptism is "indissoluble" implies not only one's eternal identity as a child of God, but God's eternal fidelity to each baptized person. Each of us will break the covenant someday—after all, part of the Baptismal Covenant reads "when [not 'if'] you fall into sin"—yet God's steadfast faithfulness to us means that the covenant holds. In his first letter to the Corinthians, Paul simply states, "God is faithful."

Have you experienced times in your life when you have either felt—or questioned—God's faithful concern for human flourishing or for your own well-being? (It's always appropriate to wrestle with God, with doubt, with faith, with honest feelings. Your willingness to confront hard questions will make you an important role model for your child or godchild. Scripture is filled with stories of men and women who questioned—even argued with—God, and remember that even in the immediate presence of Jesus, one follower cried out, "Lord, I believe; help my unbelief.")

....

....

....

....

....

....

....

....

The Rev. Dr. Carroll Simcox tells the story of how Martin Luther would deal with periods of despair or temptation: "he would take a piece of chalk and write in large letters on his desk, "I HAVE BEEN BAPTIZED" He would thus remind himself "that as a member of Christ he has given to him all the grace he needs to walk in this hard and heroic New Life.... But this above all: he is God's child forever."

What a gift you give this child, by giving him or her over to God to share in the care and love and nurture of a human soul! May it also be a blessing for you, as you renew your own Baptismal Covenant.

Take time to read once more through the whole service for Holy Baptism, beginning on page 298 with the rubrics.

Use the space below to note any final questions, concerns, or random thoughts you would like to record, either for your own pondering or to share with others as you prepare for your child's or godchild's Baptismal Day.

....

....

....

....

Part II:
Beyond Baptism

Nurturing Your Own Spirituality

In *A Place to Pray*, Roberta Bondi writes of growing up "in a home where discussing painful private matters, particularly religious ones, was thought to be more tasteless than belching at the table." I grew up "knowing" that religion and politics were unsuitable topics for polite conversation. What a hard world it sounds like for nurturing spiritual growth!

Looking back, I'm not sure that it was as stifling as it sounds because although we didn't "talk about" religion, we prayed. Even Bondi later writes that "nobody gets to know God by first intellectually working out the answers to his or her problems and then by praying, but...one gets to know God by praying." I have to admit that what I loved best about seminary was the chance to do all that talking and arguing, but what grounds me most deeply in my faith is prayer.

As an Episcopalian, I grew up hearing the language of the prayer book week by week in church, and once I got my hands on my own copy, I was able to range through it, to find already-written prayers that named my thoughts or fears or gratefulness, or that opened up new ways of seeing. How lucky I felt to have *The Book of Common Prayer* as a resource for the spiritually tongue-tied! My hope is that you, too, have a copy of the prayer book at home. (We have two upstairs, one in the study, and one in the car; I don't leave home without it....)

If you haven't explored *The Book of Common Prayer* recently, be sure to look at the "Daily Devotions for Individuals and Families" beginning on page 136, and at the "Prayers for Families and Personal Life" beginning on page 828. In *Opening the Prayer Book*, Jeffrey Lee asserts that, "The way we pray shapes what we believe." One way to nurture your own spiritual growth is through regular times of prayer at home. (And you might consider sharing those times with your spouse, and/or with your child.)

What are some remembered prayers from your own childhood? Can you still recall the words?

. . . .

. . . .

. . . .

. . . .

. . . .

. . . .

. . . .

. . . .

What is your prayer life like at this stage of your life? (Mine, when my children were young, was a mess: haphazard and fearful.)

. . . .

. . . .

. . . .

. . . .

. . . .

. . . .

The Rt. Rev. George Cadigan, retired Bishop of Missouri, speaks of "how wonderful" it is to anticipate times of prayer in which he simply talks to God. He takes pencil and paper and notes those things he wants to talk to God about.

He often begins with the "Prayer for Quiet Confidence: on page 832: *O God of peace, who hast taught us that in returning and rest we shall be saved, in quietness and confidence shall be our strength: By the might of thy Spirit lift us, we pray thee, to thy presence, where we may be still and know that thou art God....*

Or he starts with the prayer for "In the Evening" on page 833: *O Lord, support us all the day long, until the shadows lengthen, and the evening comes, and the busy world is hushed, and the fever of life is over, and our work is done. Then in your mercy, grant us a safe lodging, a holy rest, and peace at the last. Amen.*

Then he simply talks with God, and listens. Fidelity to prayer, setting aside time for intentional conversation with God and for reading one of the prayer book services, will nurture your spiritual well-being.

What are some things that, like Bishop Cadigan, you would like to talk to God about? List them—and then take some quiet time to do so.

Also, Sunday by Sunday, be sure to attend church services, to be among the gathered Body, to participate in the liturgy, to be nourished by the Word of God and by the Eucharist.

Let attendance at the Eucharist become part of the rhythm of your life. Because going to church was what I had done all my life, even when I went away to college I kept on going. (During those years I went on Wednesday mornings to a service before my first class; I did give up Sunday worship, but never church. It was too much a part of what nourished me. Find a service that feels comfortable and nourishing for your family, and be faithful participants.)

What are your current church-going habits? If you haven't been a consistent participant, can you foresee working church attendance into your life?

....

....

....

....

....

....

....

....

Suggesting regular church attendance isn't meant to sound like one more burden in your busy life, but instead is meant to be part of your spiritual self-care, a way to nurture your own ongoing relationship with God within the gathered Body of Christ, of which you are a member. By taking care of your own spiritual wellbeing, you will be better able to tend your child's or godchild's spiritual growth.

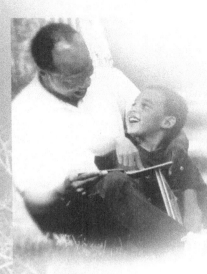

Nurturing Faith Development in Your Child

Almighty God, heavenly Father, you have blessed us with the joy and care of children: Give us calm strength and patient wisdom as we bring them up, that we may teach them to love whatever is just and true and good, following the example of our Savior Jesus Christ. Amen (from *The Book of Common Prayer*, 829).

The baptism of infants and young children places the challenge of "becoming Christian" and living into the Baptismal Covenant "with the whole church, but especially with parents and godparents," writes John Westerhoff. As the prayer above indicates, how you undertake that challenge will have profound effects on the faith development of your child or godchild.

The Rev. Paige Blair encourages parents to let their children grow up knowing about God and Jesus and the Church so that these "become part of the fabric of their consciousness." What we learn as children is literally folded into the gray matter of our brains. Westerhoff suggests "little acts such as placing a sacred image near their bed, a song softly sung while nursing, taking them to church...." I would add the suggestion that you hang the Baptismal Certificate in their room, an overt statement of their identity as baptized Christians which will be among their first visual memories.

Look around the space in which your child or godchild will sleep, whether it be the child's own room or one shared with a sibling or parent(s). Describe the space.

. . . .

. . . .

. . . .

. . . .

. . . .

. . . .

Before I can even remember, my parents had hung next to my bed
a painting of a little girl at prayer, and at the foot of my bed a print
of the women at the empty tomb. These pictures were comforting
companions from infancy until I went away to college—as were the
stuffed animals who shared my bed for many of those years. Those
things with which we surround our children (and ourselves) matter.
I remember a particularly difficult year of teaching when I hung a
copy of Edvard Munch's "The Scream" at the back of my windowless
classroom because it seemed to express my feelings. What I eventu-
ally came to realize was that daily contact with such a bleak, despairing
image exacerbated my own despair. I now have seven plants in my
room, and pastoral images of cottage doors. And before each new
school year begins, I sanctify my room with holy water.

What emotional and spiritual energy do you sense in your child's
or godchild's room? Is there anything else you want to add to the
space—or anything you wonder about removing?

. . . .

. . . .

. . . .

Ellen and Dana Charry remind us that current culture "is in many ways toxic for children and that an alternate to Hollywood, Madison Avenue, and Wall Street is urgently needed." They speak of how "Much of secular culture, which is ready to take hold of youth, is vulgar, violent, and materialistic." By starting early surrounding your child or godchild with Christian images of life and faith, with the sturdy love of family and the embrace of the Church, you give that child armor against the onslaught of culturally-imposed images and ideas that can "assault and hurt the soul."

What worries you the most as you consider watching this child grow up into today's world?

On page 829 in The *Book of Common Prayer* is a prayer "For Young Persons" to which I turn again and again, both as parent and as teacher:

> *God our Father, you see your children growing up in an*
> *unsteady and confusing world: Show them that your ways*
> *give more life than the ways of the world, and that following*

you is better than chasing after selfish goals [those "other gods" the Rev. Paige Blair speaks of].... Give them strength to hold their faith in you, and to keep alive their joy in your creation; through Jesus Christ our Lord. Amen.

Always remember that joy—abundant joy—is meant to be part of being a Christian. Despite its various dangers, the world is also filled with much that is lovely and good and worth sharing. What places, events, or activities do you look forward to sharing with this child?

....

....

....

....

....

....

....

....

Besides tending to the visual world your child or godchild encounters, you will also be a primary determiner of the child's early encounters with words. Praying with your child makes conversation with God a natural part of life. Taking your child to church lays down the language of the liturgy as part of his or her auditory world. One of my very first memories is of lying between my parents on the wooden pew at St. Matthew's in Evanston, Illinois, listening to the words of the liturgy wash over me. I credit that ongoing experience with my love not only of prayer, but of language itself.

At home, telling or reading stories from Scripture will offer a kind of "extended family" experience. "These stories have a hold on me

because they are my stories, just as they are your stories, and they are the stories of the family and community to which we belong. They make sense out of our lives, our relationships, our world, and our God. They are our true stories," writes Michael Johnston in *Engaging the Word*. Libraries and bookstores carry a wide range of picture books with Bible stories; spend time exploring them.

What are some of your own favorite stories from Scripture, either remembered from childhood or newly important?

....

....

....

....

....

....

Reading "colonize[s] the mind," says Ellen Charry. The books, not just from Scripture, that you choose for this child will become woven into his or her understanding of the world. What books, if any, does the child already have—and what are some you'd like to add to the "colony"? (A note to godparents: a carefully—prayerfully—chosen book makes an ideal gift for a godchild year by year to celebrate the anniversary of baptism.)

....

....

. . . .

. . . .

. . . .

. . . .

In her book on godparenting, Elaine Ramshaw suggests activities that parents as well as godparents might consider, such as making a scrapbook of the baptism, or decorating the baptismal candle and then lighting it each year on the anniversary of the baptism, so that the importance of being brought into the Christian family is acknowledged and celebrated.

Ramshaw also suggests giving the child a sturdy nativity set to play with, perhaps adding a new figure or animal each year.

My own children spent one long-ago Advent making a Jesse Tree, which my husband and I still have and use. Again, check libraries or bookstores for a wide range of Jesse Tree activity books. For those not familiar with the Jesse Tree, day by day during Advent it encourages the telling of different stories from Scripture, not only anchoring the Advent season in the Judeo-Christian tradition rather than in the materialistic hype of contemporary culture, but familiarizing children with many new members of "the family."

Rituals are enormously important: family rites that celebrate the seasons, grace before meals, times of daily prayer. What are some of your own childhood memories of the various holiday seasons and celebrations? Which do you hope to pass on to this child?

. . . .

. . . .

. . . .

What are other memories of family rites, religious or otherwise, repeated behaviors that helped define family life while you were growing up?

....
....
....
....
....
....
....
....

Draw or describe your childhood image or understanding of God.

Is this still the concept you retain? If not, how is it different and when did it change?

. . . .

. . . .

. . . .

. . . .

. . . .

. . . .

What is your deepest longing for your child's or godchild's spiritual growth, for his or her image or understanding of God?

. . . .

. . . .

. . . .

. . . .

. . . .

. . . .

Besides some of the ways suggested here, what are other ways you would like to foster the faith development and spiritual wellbeing of this child?

. . . .

. . . .

. . . .

. . . .

. . . .

Trying to plan for the spiritual wellbeing and faith development of a child can feel daunting, which is why the companionship of the wider church community is so helpful. "We need to know that our children are in God's hands and that we are not alone in our love for them," writes Westerhoff. You, as well as your child or godchild, are part of the Christian community.

"Christians who accept the Christian life are never alone, or left to fend for themselves" says Charry. "They are always accompanied by the cross of Christ, their baptism, and the Holy Spirit, and resocialized by public practices and a strong community ethos that reinforces their identity."

Always be open to asking God's help, as well as the help of your brothers and sisters in Christ, as you negotiate the joyful, harrowing upbringing of this beloved child.

> *May God the Father, who by Baptism adopts us as his children, grant you grace. Amen.*
>
> *May God the Son, who sanctified a home in Nazareth, fill you with love. Amen.*
>
> *May God the Holy Spirit, who has made the Church one family, keep you in peace. Amen.*
>
> (from "A Thanksgiving for the Birth or Adoption of a Child" in *The Book of Common Prayer*, pp. 443-445)

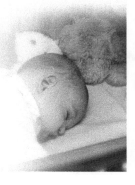

Bibliography

Arthur, Ginny, Stephen Hopkins and Margaret Murray. *Talking about Baptism.* Toronto: Anglican Book Centre, 1998.

Bondi, Roberta. *A Place to Pray.* Nashville: Abingdon Press, 1998.

The Book of Common Prayer. New York: Oxford University Press, 1990.

The Book of Occasional Services. New York: Church Publishing Inc., 1995.

Charry, Ellen. *By the Renewing of Your Minds.* New York: Oxford University Press, 1997.

Charry, Ellen and Dana Charry. "Send a Christian to Camp." *The Christian Century* vol.116:20. 14-21 July, 1999: 708-710.

Children's Charter for the Church.

Common Worship: Services and Prayers for the Church of England. London: Church House Publishing, 2000.

Eastman, A. Theodore. *The Baptizing Community.* Harrisburg PA: Morehouse Publishing, 1991.

Griswold, Frank T. "The Easter Mystery." *Episcopal Life.* June 2001: 19.

Griswold, Frank T. "The Journey of Growing up into Christ." *Episcopal Life.* May 2001: 14.

Griswold, Frank T. "The Spirit brings us nearer to Christ." *Episcopal Life.* July/ August 2001: 17.

Hines, John M. *By Water and the Holy Spirit.* New York: The Seabury Press, 1973.

Johnston, Michael. *Engaging the Word: The Church's New Teaching Series* vol. 3. Cambridge: Cowley Publications, 1998.

Lee, Jeffrey. *Opening the Prayer Book: The Church's New Teaching Series* vol. 7. Cambridge: Cowley Publications, 1999.

Micks, Marianne. *Deep Waters: An Introduction to Baptism.* Cambridge: Cowley Publications, 1996.

Mitchell, Leonel L. *Praying Shapes Believing: a Theological Commentary on the Book of Common Prayer*. Minneapolis: Winston Press, 1985.

National Children's Unit Anglican Church of Canada. *A Gift for the Journey: A Baptismal Preparation Kit*. Toronto: Anglican Book Centre, 1993.

O'Day, Gail R. "The Gospel of John: Introduction, Commentary, and Reflections." *The New Interpreter's Bible* vol. IX. Nashville: Abingdon Press, 1995.

Portaro, Sam. *Crossing the Jordan*. Cambridge: Cowley Publications, 1999.

Ramshaw, Elaine. *The Godparent Book*. Chicago: Liturgy Training Publications, 1993.

Romero, Oscar. *The Violence of Love*. Compiled and trans. James R. Brockman, SJ. Farmington PA: The Plough Publishing House, 1998.

Simcox, Carroll E. *Understanding the Sacraments*. New York: Morehouse-Gorham Co., 1956.

Southcott, Ernest. *Receive This Child*. London: R. Mowbray & Co., Limited, 1951.

Stevick, Daniel B. *Baptismal Moments; Baptismal Meanings*. New York: The Church Hymnal Corporation, 1987.

Tammany, Klara. *Living Water: Baptism as a Way of Life*. New York: Church Publishing Incorporated, 2002.

Taylor, Barbara Brown. *The Preaching Life*. Cambridge: Cowley Publications, 1993.

Weil, Louis. *A Theology of Worship*. Cambridge: Cowley Publications, 2002.

Westerhoff, John H. *Holy Baptism: A Guide for Parents and Godparents*. Atlanta: The Institute for Pastoral Study, St. Luke's Press, 1996.

Willimon, William H. *What's Right with the Church?* San Francisco: Harper & Row, 1985.

www.ingramcontent.com/pod-product-compliance
Lightning Source LLC
Jackson TN
JSHW011943131224
75386JS00041B/1550